4TH GRADE
ENGLISH AND LANGUAGE ARTS

Unit 5

Table of Contents

ResponsiveEd® thanks Character First (www.characterfirst.com) for permission to integrate its character resources into this Unit.

Objectives

- Explain the roles and functions of characters in a story.
- Differentiate between a character's emotions and character traits.
- Understand how characters develop in a story.
- Understand relationships between characters in a story.
- Understand sequence and plot development in *In the Year of the Boar and Jackie Robinson* and *Dear Austin*.
- Identify the meaning of idioms.
- Use Greek and Latin roots to determine the meanings of unknown words.
- Write an IAM poem using a character from either *In the Year of the Boar and Jackie Robinson* or *Dear Austin*.
- Use comparative and superlative adjectives and adverbs correctly.
- Understand how to compare and contrast.
- Improve metaphors with adjectives.
- Make literary connections between two texts.
- Compare and contrast characters from two texts.
- Determine the point of view of a narrator.
- Write a compare and contrast five-paragraph essay.
- Write detailed sentences.
- Understand how setting contributes to the plot of a story.
- Revise your compare and contrast essay.
- Edit your work and the work of others.
- Spell homophones and words that end with *–ure* correctly.
- Complete analogies using synonyms and antonyms.
- Publish your writing.

Throughout this course, you will read at least 20 minutes four times during the week. Then, you will write a response in a Reading Journal.

You will need a composition book or spiral notebook. On the cover, label it "Reading Journal" and write your name on it.

OBJECTIVES

- Explain the roles and functions of characters in a story.
- Differentiate between a character's emotions and character traits.
- Understand how characters develop in a story.
- Understand relationships between characters in a story.
- Understand sequence and plot development in *In the Year of the Boar and Jackie Robinson* and *Dear Austin*.
- Identify the meaning of idioms.
- Use Greek and Latin roots to determine the meanings of unknown words.
- Write an IAM poem using a character from either *In the Year of the Boar and Jackie Robinson* or *Dear Austin*.
- Use comparative and superlative adjectives and adverbs correctly.

VOCABULARY

characters *[KAR-ik-terz]* – (noun) people or animals in stories

conflict *[KON-flikt]* – (noun) a struggle between two opposing forces that brings change to a story

external *[ik-STUR-nl]* **conflict** – (noun) conflict that happens between a character and outside forces such as nature, a physical obstacle, or another character

internal *[in-TUR-nl]* **conflict** – (noun) conflict that happens inside of a character

main character – (noun) the most important character in the story

minor character – (noun) a character that plays a role in the story but is not as important as the main character

1. CHARACTER DEVELOPMENT

CHARACTER ROLES AND CONFLICT

Characters are the people (or animals) in stories. The **main character** is the most important character in the story. **Minor characters** also play a role in the story, but they are not as important as the main character. **Conflict** happens when the main character interacts with the minor characters. When a conflict occurs in a story, the personality of the main character comes out. More is learned about the main character as a result of the conflict or conflicts.

Main character from *In the Year of the Boar and Jackie Robinson*:

- Shirley Temple Wong

Examples of some minor characters from *In the Year of the Boar and Jackie Robinson*:

- Mother
- Father
- Mabel
- Emily

Main character from *Dear Austin*:

- Levi Ives

Examples of minor characters from *Dear Austin*:

- Jupiter
- Darcy
- Possum
- Miss Amelia

There are two types of conflicts that characters face. One type of conflict is called **external conflict**. The second type of conflict is called **internal conflict**.

External Conflict

- Two characters battle each other. (man versus man)
- The main character struggles against a belief that the majority of the community and/or surroundings believes. (man versus society)
- The main character battles nature. (man versus nature)

Internal Conflict

- The main character battles an inner emotion such as fear. (man versus him/herself)
- The main character wants something, but in order to get it, he or she must do something that they believe is wrong. (man versus him/herself)

Characters face both external and internal conflicts. That's what makes characters realistic. It also makes books interesting and enjoyable to read.

Just as in real life, characters undergo changes as a result of the conflicts they face. In our two books, both main characters faced internal and external conflicts throughout the story.

Shirley's Conflicts

Examples of External Conflicts:

- Shirley versus Awaiting Marriage (servant)
- Shirley versus the students in the fifth grade
- Shirley versus Mabel

Examples of Internal Conflicts:

- Shirley versus her fear of acceptance by new classmates
- Shirley versus her loneliness
- Shirley versus keeping her Chinese heritage alive

Levi's Conflicts

Examples of External Conflicts:

- Levi versus the bull
- Levi versus dance lessons
- Levi versus slave catchers

Examples of Internal Conflicts:

- Levi versus his guilt over how Mrs. Simpson treated Darcy
- Levi versus his fear of not knowing where Darcy was
- Levi versus his nightmares

CHARACTER TRAITS

Character traits are the qualities of a certain character and can be physical or emotional. Emotional traits help to make up a character's personality. You can learn a character's personality through their *actions*, *thoughts*, and *feelings*. You can learn about a character's physical traits by the way the author describes them or things that they say or do. Some examples of physical traits are a character's height, hair length, hair color, and eye color.

Character-trait words are adjectives because they describe people, a type of noun. Read through the list of words that describe character traits. For a longer or more extensive list of character traits, you may use the internet to find lists. You can type in "character traits list" in the search engine. As always, be sure to get permission before going on the internet.

Honest	Courageous	Loyal	Simple-minded
Inspiring	Compassionate	Energetic	Selfish
Brave	Proud	Prim	Independent
Mischievous	Curious	Responsible	Fun-loving
Disagreeable	Hard-working	Patriotic	Bossy
Thoughtful	Adventurous	Tall	Serious
Fancy	Bold	Short	Humble
Gentle	Daring	Handsome	Tough

You will need both of your books on hand to compete the next activity. You will include specific examples and text evidence from the books to analyze the character traits of the two main characters. An example has been done for the character Mabel from *In the Year of the Boar and Jackie Robinson*.

Example: Read the completed graphic organizer on Character Trait Analysis.

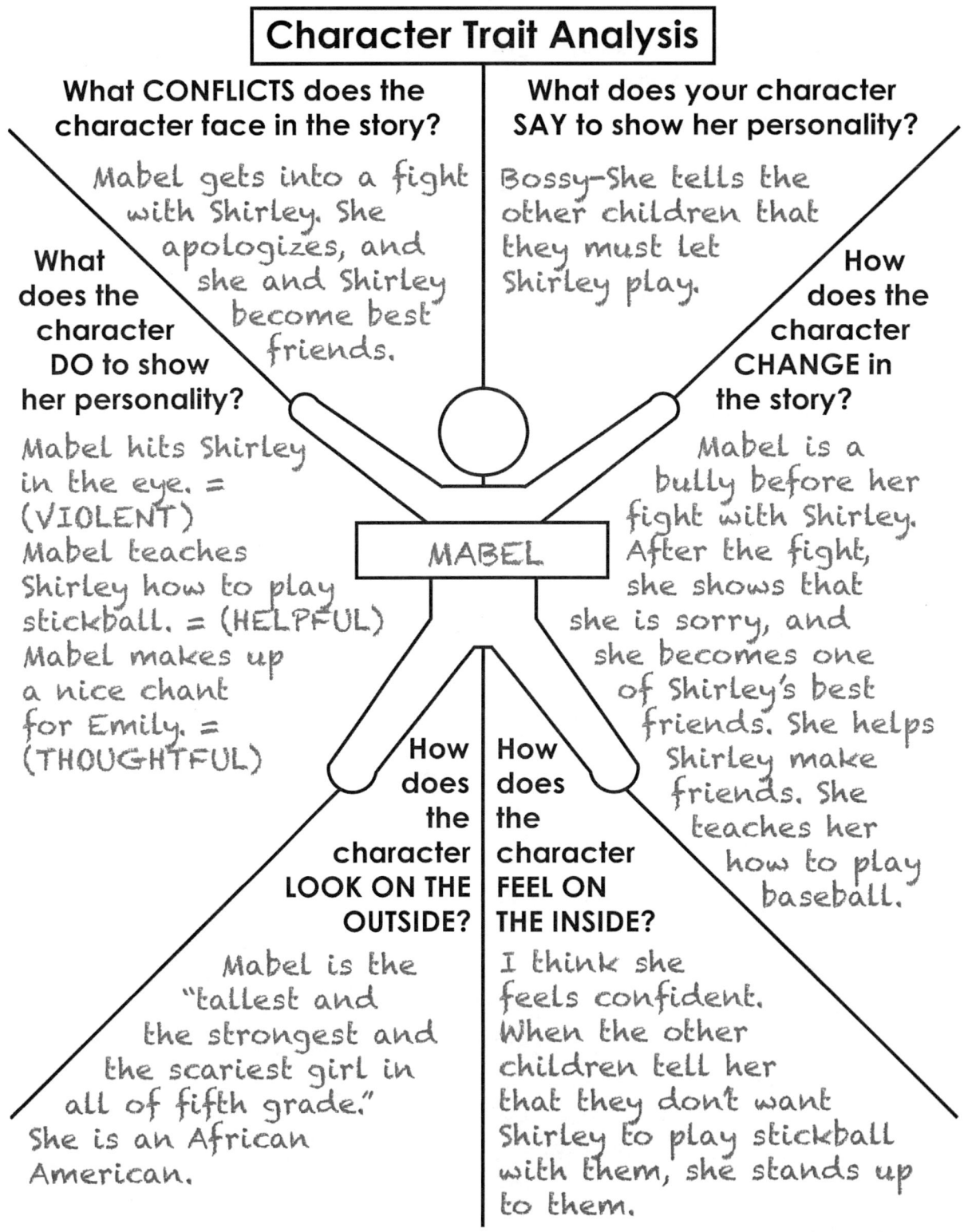

Character Trait Analysis

What CONFLICTS does the character face in the story?

Mabel gets into a fight with Shirley. She apologizes, and she and Shirley become best friends.

What does your character SAY to show her personality?

Bossy-She tells the other children that they must let Shirley play.

What does the character DO to show her personality?

Mabel hits Shirley in the eye. = (VIOLENT)
Mabel teaches Shirley how to play stickball. = (HELPFUL)
Mabel makes up a nice chant for Emily. = (THOUGHTFUL)

How does the character CHANGE in the story?

Mabel is a bully before her fight with Shirley. After the fight, she shows that she is sorry, and she becomes one of Shirley's best friends. She helps Shirley make friends. She teaches her how to play baseball.

MABEL

How does the character LOOK ON THE OUTSIDE?

Mabel is the "tallest and the strongest and the scariest girl in all of fifth grade." She is an African American.

How does the character FEEL ON THE INSIDE?

I think she feels confident. When the other children tell her that they don't want Shirley to play stickball with them, she stands up to them.

Complete a character trait analysis chart for the main characters in each of the novels you have read. Create one for Shirley and one for Levi. There are six areas on each worksheet. Write down information about the two characters in these six areas. After you have finished, color and decorate the graphic organizers.

Here are the questions that guide the information you should put in each of the six areas:

1 – What **conflicts** does the character face? Choose three examples of conflicts that the character faces in the story. Include information on how the character overcomes each challenge.

2 – What does the character **say** to show his/her personality? You have two options for this question. Option 1: Find quotes from the characters that show why you used the words from #1 to describe him/her. Option 2: Choose three more character-trait words that you feel describe your character. Think of what the character says to make you describe him/her that way. Write this information in one of the areas on the graphic organizer.

3 – How does the character **change** in the story? Explain how the character changes in the book. Consider how you would have described him/her in the beginning of the story and how you would describe him/her at the end.

4 – How does the character **feel on the inside**? Explain what you have learned about how the character feels on the inside. Use evidence from the book on how the author describes him/her. Think about the things you have learned about them from the dialogue and action.

5 – How does the character **look on the outside**? Explain what you have learned about what the character looks like. Use evidence from the book on how the author describes him/her. Think about the things you have learned about the character from the dialogue and action.

6 – What does the character **do** to show his/her personality? Choose three words that describe the character from the character trait list or your own list. Think of what the character does to make you describe him/her that way. Write this information in one of the areas on the graphic organizer.

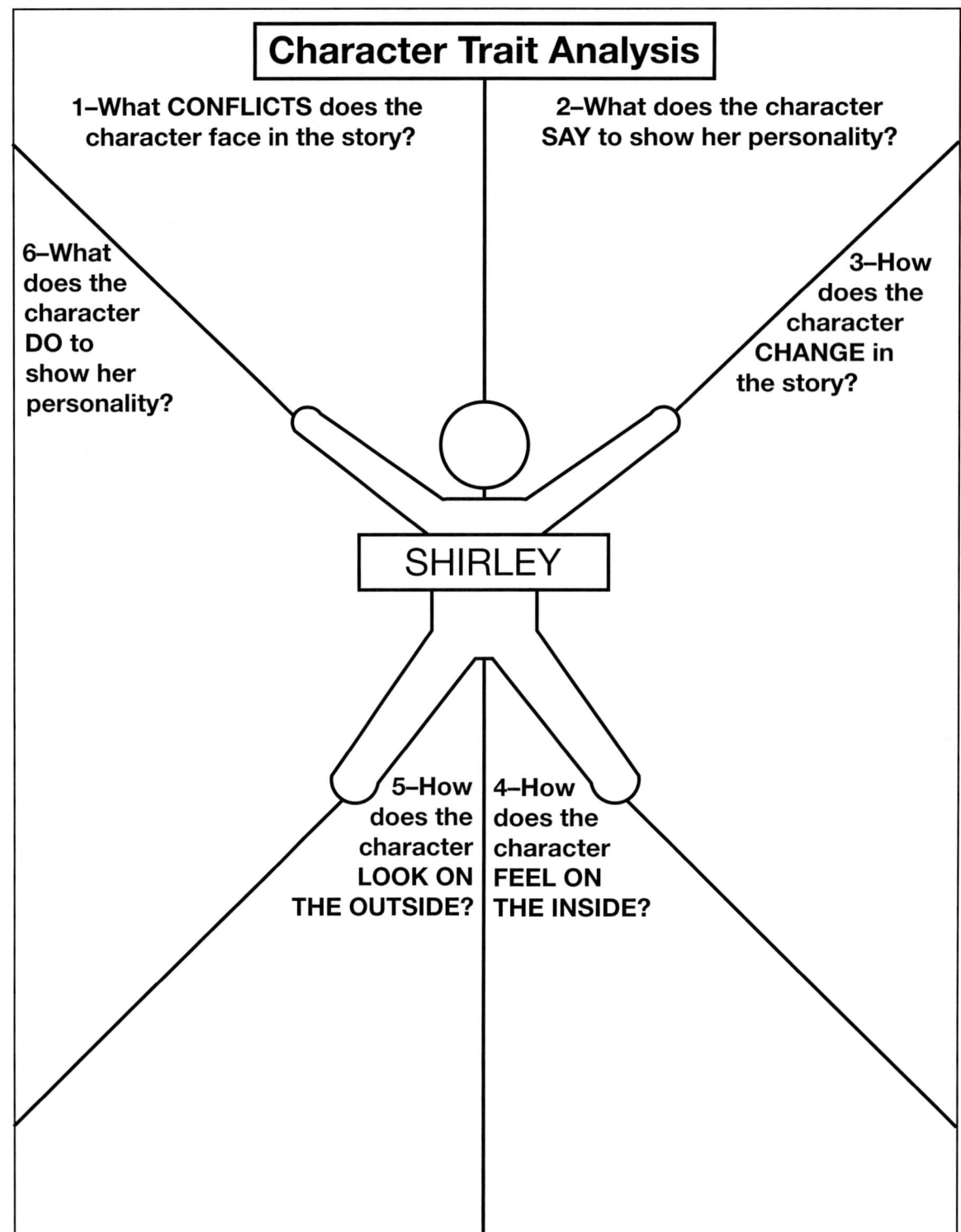

Character Trait Analysis

1–What CONFLICTS does the character face in the story?

2–What does the character SAY to show her personality?

6–What does the character DO to show her personality?

3–How does the character CHANGE in the story?

SHIRLEY

5–How does the character LOOK ON THE OUTSIDE?

4–How does the character FEEL ON THE INSIDE?

1.2)

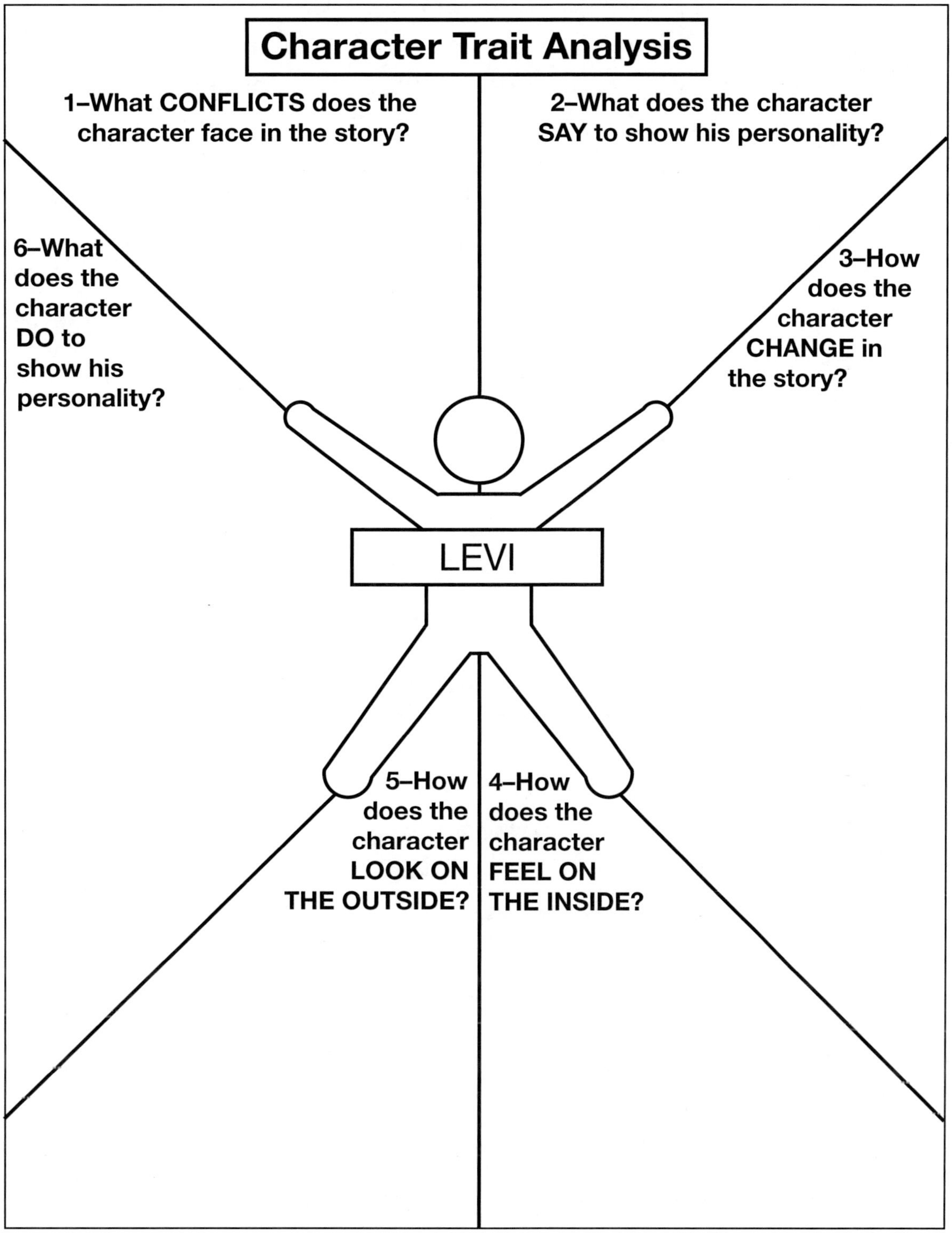

Character Trait Analysis

1–What CONFLICTS does the character face in the story?

2–What does the character SAY to show his personality?

6–What does the character DO to show his personality?

3–How does the character CHANGE in the story?

LEVI

5–How does the character LOOK ON THE OUTSIDE?

4–How does the character FEEL ON THE INSIDE?

Teacher Check

CHARACTER DEVELOPMENT

Did you notice that both Shirley and Levi change in the story? Each character has a series of conflicts that reveal a little more of their traits. With each new conflict, the main character has to work through the conflict and is changed as a result. Do you know the story called *A Christmas Carol* by Charles Dickens? The main character, Scrooge, is a mean, old, greedy man who does not understand or appreciate the Christmas spirit. After he is forced to face some conflicts, he becomes a changed man. He learns to have the Christmas spirit— to be kind, warm, generous, and giving. His character develops (changes) throughout the course of the story, just as the characters Shirley and Levi change.

For this next activity, choose one major conflict from the Conflict Box that the main character in each book had to face. You will write about how the main character changes as a result of the conflict. Write the page number(s) to support your answers as text evidence.

Conflict Box

Shirley's Conflicts:
- Her loneliness (learning to adapt to a new language and culture while missing her extended family in China)
- Her fight with Mabel
- Replacing the money spent instead of saving it (babysitting)

Levi's Conflicts:
- His nightmares
- Trying to find Darcy
- His sense of justice towards slavery (learning about the injustice of slavery, the need for the Underground Railroad, and the importance of meeting Harriet Tubman)

1.3) Fill in the chart.

Shirley

Conflict: Write a major conflict the main character must face.

Goal: What is the main character's goal to get through this conflict?

Outcome: How does the main character change, or what lesson is learned?

Levi

Conflict: Write a major conflict the main character must face.

Goal: What is the main character's goal to get through this conflict?

Outcome: How does the main character change, or what lesson is learned?

 Teacher Check

9

2. PLOT DEVELOPMENT

You have already learned about the plot diagram from Unit 1. Remember, the plot diagram consists of the following: exposition/introduction, rising action, climax, falling action, and the resolution/conclusion.

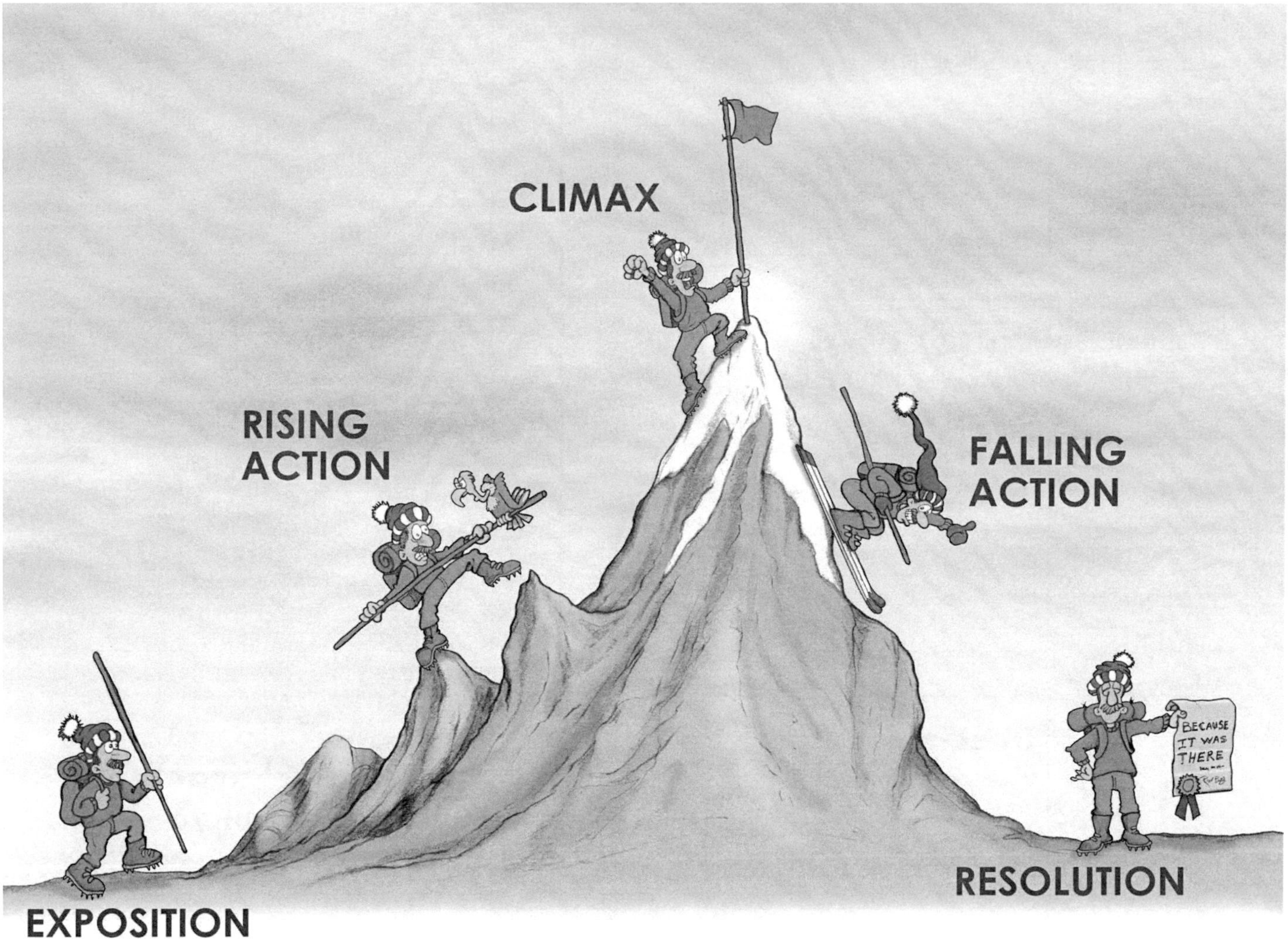

CLIMAX

RISING ACTION

FALLING ACTION

EXPOSITION

RESOLUTION

Most stories will have more than one conflict within the story to help develop the plot. With each new conflict, the main character will also reveal another character trait about himself or herself. The development of the plot moves the story along and helps to keep the reader's attention.

Number the events 1–6 in the order that they happened in each book. You may write the numbers anywhere in each box.

2.1) *Dear Austin—Letters From the Underground Railroad*

The boys run into Harriet Tubman.	Jupiter jumps off Widow's Rock to prevent Harvey from dropping his dog off the bank.
We learn the year this story takes place is in 1853.	Darcy receives the walking stick with the nightingale carved in at the top of the stick.
Levi learns that Miss Ameila is working with the Underground Railroad.	Jupiter and Levi are lost in the woods.

Shirley gets a new American name.

Shirley is admitted into her local school as a fifth grader instead of a third grader.

We learn the year this story takes place is in 1947.

Shirley gains a new friend, Emily Levy.

Shirley gains the respect and friendship of Mabel and then, her classmates.

Shirley presents the key to her school to Jackie Robinson, her favorite baseball player.

Check   Correct   Recheck

MORE IDIOMS

Today, you will learn four more idioms. Read the idioms and their meanings, and then complete the activity.

Idioms

- *Two wrongs don't make a right.*—You cannot correct one wrong thing by doing something else that is wrong.

- *Through thick and thin*—to go through the good times (thick) and the bad times (thin)

- *When it rains, it pours.*—Something that starts out as a little bit of trouble turns into a disaster.

- *Beat around the bush*—used when someone is avoiding the main point in a conversation

Fill in the blanks in the story with the four idioms you learned in this Lesson.

My cousin, Rachel, came running into the room and said, "I've got something important to tell you."

I said, "Okay. Let me have it."

Rachel said, "You might want to sit down for this."

I answered, "Okay. I'm going to sit down."

Rachel continued, "You know you're my favorite cousin, right?"

I answered, "Yes."

She said, "And I love you more than anything, right?"

I said, "Rachel, don't 2.3) _____;
just tell me already!"

She said, "Well, Jennifer told Tommy that she's not going to be able to be in the talent show this weekend."

"What?" I yelled. "Why not?" I asked, trying to remain calm. I thought to myself, Jennifer is the second person to drop out of this week's show.

2.4) _____!

13

Rachel said, "Jennifer told Tommy that she's going to Laura's party instead. I guess you guys aren't as close as you thought. I mean, you guys have been friends for years, ever since kindergarten. I can't believe she'd pull a stunt like this. You guys have been 2.5) _____ together. What are you going to do? I would stop being her best friend if I were you."

I answered, "Yes, we have been best friends for a long time, ten years to be exact. No, I'm not going to stop being friends with her. You know, 2.6) _____. Instead, I'm going to call her and see what's going on. Better still, I'm going over to her house to talk with her right now."

MORE GREEK AND LATIN ROOTS

Recognizing Greek and Latin roots will help you to figure out the meanings of new or unfamiliar words. The Latin root *scrib* or *scrip* means "write." The Greek root *log* means "word," "speech," and "study." Read and study the meanings of each word. If you do not know the meaning of a word, look it up in the dictionary.

Latin root *scrib* or *scrip*

inscribe
prescription
transcribe
manuscript

Greek root *log*

biology
dialogue
monologue
technology

Fill in the blanks using words that have the Latin roots *scrib* or *scrip* and the Greek root *log*.

2.7) After my little sister was seen by the doctor, she was given a(n) _____ for medicine.

2.8) Ancient scholars _____ important documents to keep copies and records for safekeeping.

2.9) My mother has beautiful handwriting skills. Her _____ is so nice; it looks like my teacher's handwriting!

2.10) _____ is constantly changing and advancing. Today's smartphone will be considered old in just a couple of years from now.

2.11) Shakespeare wrote many plays where some characters have a(n) _____, a short speech.

2.12) The words that are exchanged between actors or characters in a play, drama, or story is called the _____.

2.13) Steven has been studying about cells in his _____ class.

2.14) The author will _____ the book with his signature.

Check   Correct   Recheck

3. IAM POEM

Writing

IAM POEM

Have you ever heard of an IAM poem? You can use an IAM poem to show what you learn about characters in stories that you read. You are going to write an IAM poem about one of your favorite characters from one of the two novels you've just read. You will write the poem as if you were that character. Include details that you learned about the character as well as inferences you made about the personality of the character.

The IAM poem has 18 lines and is told in first-person point of view, so every line begins with the Word *I* and a verb. Each line has specific information about the character. Lines 1, 6, 12, and 18 repeat *I am*. In those lines there is a choice. The first option is to repeat the same line each time. The other option is to write a different line each time as you will see in the example.

Read the following example. The character is from a story you have already read and learned about in Unit 1 called *Black Beauty*. Ginger was a horse that was one of Black Beauty's friends. Read the IAM poem about Ginger.

Ginger

1   I am proud and beautiful

2   I wonder why I am mistreated by some human beings

3   I hear the thundering of hooves across grassy meadows

4   I see Black Beauty ready to take his Mistress to the park

5   I want freedom to run and stretch my legs

6   I am weary

7   I pretend to be happy and hopeful for a better future

8   I feel worried about my future

9   I touch my muzzle next to Black Beauty's for comfort and encouragement

10   I worry for Black Beauty's future too

11   I cry on the inside

12   I am tired

13   I understand my place in this world

14   I say one day I will be free

15   I dream of sunshine, running with my friends, and freedom

16   I try to stay obedient to my Master

17   I hope for a better future for the younger foals and fillies

18   I am free now

3.1) Write an IAM poem using a character from either *In the Year of the Boar and Jackie Robinson* or *Dear Austin*.

_____

I am_____
I wonder_____
I hear_____
I see_____
I want_____
I am_____
I pretend_____
I feel_____
I touch_____
I worry_____
I cry_____
I am_____
I understand_____
I say_____
I dream_____
I try_____
I hope_____
I am_____

Teacher Check

IAM POEM RUBRIC

	4 Points	3 Points	2 Points	1 Point	Point Tally
Focus and Coherence	The poem as a whole is focused. It has a sense of completeness. The poet's tone is evident.	The poem is mostly focused. It has a sense of completeness. The poet's tone is mostly evident.	The poem is somewhat focused. It seems incomplete. The poet's tone is somewhat evident.	The ideas presented seem random and disconnected. The poet's tone is not evident.	_____
Voice	The poem is creative and original. The poet uniquely expresses his or her ideas and emotions.	The poem is thoughtful and creative. The overall product is carefully written.	Most of the poem is creative but appears to be rushed.	The poem appears to be rushed. The ideas are not original.	_____
Content of Poem— Point of View— First Person	The poet follows the format for each line of the poem. The poem expresses an in-depth understanding of the character.	The poet follows the format for each line of the poem. The poem expresses a mostly clear understanding of the character.	The poet follows the format for most of the poem. The poem expresses a somewhat clear understanding of the character.	The poet follows the format for less than half of the poem. The poem does not express a clear understanding of the character.	_____
Development of Ideas	The development of the poem is thoughtful and engaging because specific, well-chosen details are included.	The development of the poem reflects some thoughtfulness.	The development of the poem is minimal because there are few details, or they are too general.	The development of the poem is weak because the details are inappropriate, vague, or insufficient.	_____

Conventions	The poem has grade-level appropriate spelling, grammar, and punctuation; it contains few, if any, errors that interfere with the reader's understanding.	The poem has mainly grade-level appropriate spelling, grammar, and punctuation; it contains 1–2 errors, but they do not interfere with the reader's understanding.	The poem may contain 3–4 errors in spelling, grammar, and/ or punctuation that may interfere with the reader's understanding.	The poem may contain frequent and numerous errors (5+) in spelling, grammar, and punctuation that interfere with the reader's understanding.	
					_____
Total Points =					_____
Grade (This assignment is worth 100 points.) **Total Points (_____) × 5 =**					_____

COMPARATIVE AND SUPERLATIVE ADJECTIVES AND ADVERBS

In Unit 2, you were introduced to superlative and comparative words. This chart shows a few more examples of the comparative and superlative adjective forms.

COMPARATIVE AND SUPERLATIVE FORMS

Base Form	Comparative Form	Superlative Form
fast	faster	fastest
dark	darker	darkest
small	smaller	smallest
high	higher	highest
honest	more honest	most honest
intelligent	more intelligent	most intelligent

*Hint: Do not use *more*, *most*, *less*, or *least* before adjectives that already end with
–er or –est. This is called a double comparison.

Example sentence: Jupiter was ***braver*** than Possum. (comparative form)

Example sentence: Levi was the ***bravest*** of them all. (superlative form)

Review

Underline the best answers.

3.2) The skyscraper on the left was (**tall, taller**) than the skyscraper on the right.

3.3) Harley is (**bigger, big**) than Jupiter.

3.4) I always draw (**straight, straighter**) lines with a ruler than without one.

3.5) Of all the family members, Mother wakes up the (**earlier, earliest**) in the mornings.

3.6) Brandon came too (**late, later**), so he missed the sign-up deadline for the event.

3.7) Shirley listened to the radio (**little, less**) in the winter.

3.8) Shirley was the (**smaller, smallest**) student in her fifth-grade class.

3.9) Mabel is (**funnier, funniest**) than Tommy.

3.10) Jackie Robinson is one of the (**more popular, most popular**) baseball players of all time.

QUIZ 1

(Each answer, 5 points)
Match the idioms with the descriptions.

1.01) _____ *When it rains, it pours.*

1.02) _____ *Two wrongs don't make a right.*

1.03) _____ *through thick and thin*

1.04) _____ *beat around the bush*

A. to go through good times and bad times

B. when someone is avoiding the main point in a conversation

C. You cannot correct one wrong thing by doing something else that is wrong.

D. Something that starts out as a little bit of trouble turns into a disaster.

Fill in the blanks using idioms from the box below.

Two wrongs don't make a right	through thick and thin
beat around the bush	When it rains, it pours

1.05) It bothers my mom when I _____ instead of just telling her what I want.

1.06) My brother and I are best friends. We have been

_____ with each other.

1.07) My grandfather says, "_____" when we try to get revenge on each other.

1.08) First, the tire on my bike was flat. Next, I realized that I forgot to let the dog out. Then, I stepped into a puddle outside the library.

_____!

Fill in the blanks using words from the box below.

| inscribe | manuscript | monologue | prescription |
| biology | technology | transcribe | dialogue |

1.09) Authors use _____ to help readers understand characters' traits.

1.010) The doctor gave me a(n) _____ that would help me get over my ear infection.

1.011) My brother is studying _____ in college because he wants to be a doctor.

1.012) I won a trophy, and they will _____ my name on the front of it.

1.013) Some people prefer to type their assignments, but I prefer to use _____.

1.014) My grandmother says that she doesn't understand how to use all of the new _____ in order to text on the phone.

Write T for True or F for False.

1.015) _____ You can use *more*, *most*, *less*, or *least* with words that already end in –er or –est.

1.016) _____ Superlative words end in –est and comparative words end in –er.

Underline the best answers.

1.017) Who is the (**taller**, **tallest**) boy in the fifth-grade class?

1.018) Hummingbirds are the (**most beautiful**, **beautifulest**) birds in the world.

1.019) I arrived at the party (**earlier**, **more early**) than my cousin, Tammy.

1.020) Jane thinks that writing poetry is (**easier**, **easiest**) than writing stories.

Check ☐   Correct ☐   Recheck ☐

SECTION TWO

OBJECTIVES

- Understand how to compare and contrast.
- Improve metaphors with adjectives.
- Make literary connections between two texts.
- Compare and contrast characters from two texts.
- Determine the point of view of a narrator.
- Write a compare and contrast five-paragraph essay.

VOCABULARY

compare *[kuhm-PAIR]* – (verb) to examine two or more things and identify their similarities

contrast *[kon-TRAST]* – (verb) to examine two or more things and identify their differences

4. COMPARE AND CONTRAST

COMPARE AND CONTRAST

When you compare and contrast things, you look for the similarities and differences between them. **Compare** means to see how things or ideas are similar, or alike, to one another. To **contrast** is to see how things or ideas are different from one another.

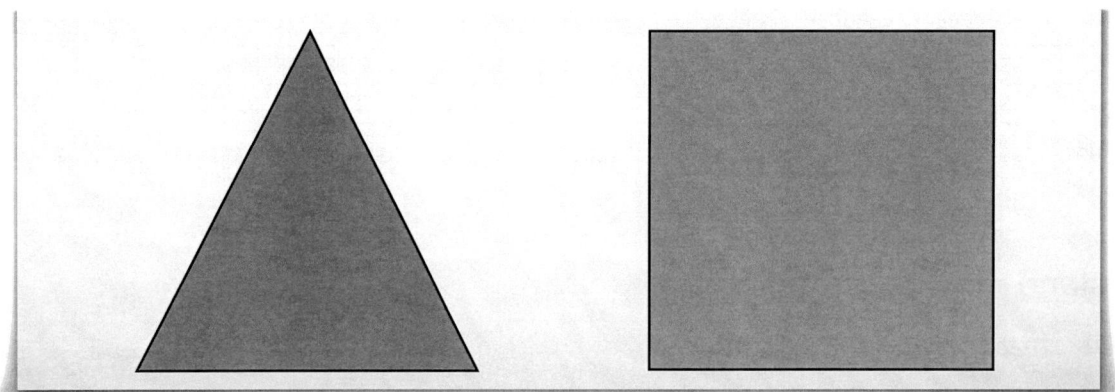

Compare: A *square and a triangle are similar because they are both shapes.*

Contrast: *A square and a triangle are different because a triangle has three sides and a square has four sides.*

Review

Write a sentence explaining how each pair of words are similar. Use complete sentences. Use your best cursive handwriting.

4.1) carrots   beets

_____

4.2) violin   flute

_____

4.3) bicycle   truck

_____

4.4) dog   cat

_____

4.5) pencil   pen

_____

Write a sentence explaining how each pair of words are different. Use complete sentences.

4.6) computer   tablet

_____

4.7) dining table office desk

_____

4.8) novel   short story

_____

4.9) scissors   knife

_____

4.10) backpack   purse

_____

 **Teacher Check** ☐

 These spelling words are all related to comparing and contrasting. Read each word and say it aloud.

4.11) Write the spelling words five times each on separate paper.

compare	similarity
differently	differences
comparison	similarly
similar	different
differ	similarities

Note: You will be tested on all of the spelling words during the Unit Test.

 **Teacher Check** ☐

Your spelling words come from three base words: *compare*, *differ*, and *similar*. The other seven words are variations of these three base words.

Word	Part of speech	How to use it in a sentence
compare	verb	I asked my mom not to **compare** me to my older brother because it made me uncomfortable.
comparison	noun	Our assignment requires us to make a **comparison** of the two main characters.
differ	verb	How does baseball **differ** from softball?
different	adjective	Although they are twins, Brad and Joe are **different** from each other.
differences	noun (plural)	There are only a few **differences** between playing baseball and softball.
differently	adverb	I decided to draw this picture **differently** than I did the first one.
similar	adjective	It was easy to see how the twins were **similar**.
similarity	noun (singular)	There is only one **similarity** between the two boys.

similarly	adverb	It was hard to figure it out because John and Janet write *similarly*.
similarities	noun (plural)	There are few *similarities* between the two boys.

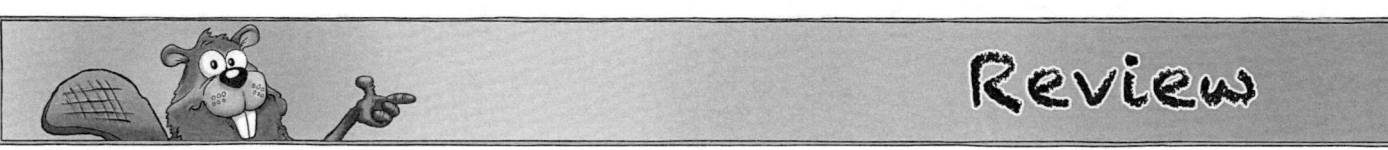

Review

Underline the forms of the words that best complete the sentences.

4.12) You can use a Venn diagram to list all of the (**similar**, **similarities**) and (**differ**, **differences**) between the two stories we read.

4.13) The twins look (**similarly**, **similar**), but they behave (**different**, **differently**).

4.14) I had to (**compare**, **comparison**) the two bats to decide which one I liked better.

4.15) I didn't realize how many (**different**, **differences**) kinds of apples there are.

4.16) A (**similarities**, **similarity**) that Glen and I share is that we both have two brothers.

4.17–4.22) Find the spelling words in the word search puzzle.

| differences | different | differently | similar | similarity | similarly |

Compare and Contrast Words

```
S  E  S  Z  J  V  D  U  C  J  S  I  U  J  Y
I  Y  E  Q  B  G  K  I  I  I  A  Z  J  L  A
M  M  C  E  D  X  T  W  M  V  R  Z  T  O  U
I  Z  N  R  Z  Q  P  I  V  X  T  N  T  X  G
L  E  E  D  C  K  L  N  L  K  E  F  C  B  Y
A  W  R  I  I  A  T  W  J  R  N  N  V  V  F
R  L  E  D  R  F  U  W  E  B  U  P  P  V  Y
L  Y  F  G  X  T  F  F  W  W  D  C  V  B  K
Y  A  F  E  Z  B  F  E  A  Q  K  R  V  J  Y
E  I  I  A  R  I  Z  U  R  D  D  Q  H  T  C
J  L  D  L  D  C  L  H  G  E  A  A  P  E  V
S  I  M  I  L  A  R  I  T  Y  N  B  H  W  S
V  B  L  J  A  M  Q  P  Y  B  C  T  E  D  S
R  X  D  O  Y  X  I  W  R  E  K  C  Q  N  V
O  H  P  N  Z  U  E  Z  M  Y  T  K  X  T  K
```

IMPROVING METAPHORS WITH ADJECTIVES

Do you recall what a metaphor is? It compares two things that are NOT alike without using *like* or *as*. For example, read the following sentence: *Her eyes were sparkling diamonds.* The writer knows that her eyes are not really diamonds. By comparing her eyes to the likeness of how diamonds sparkle, the reader knows that her eyes seem to twinkle and shine. In that sentence, can you identify the adjective? Look at the sentence again.

Example: *Her eyes were **sparkling** diamonds.*

Today, you will be practicing adding adjectives to metaphors. This exercise will help you to improve both your skills in identifying and understanding metaphors, as well as using adjectives in your writing.

> adjectives – words that describe nouns or pronouns

How do we make our sentences more interesting and dynamic? We can change or add an adjective to deepen or strengthen the meaning of a sentence. Read sentence 1. It is a metaphor.

Sentence 1: *She is a statue.*

Sentence 1 compares "she" to a statue. What might you infer about her from that sentence? Maybe she is stiff in the way she stands. Maybe she doesn't have feelings.

Sentence 2: *She is a **cold**, **stone** statue.*

However, in sentence 2, the adjectives *cold* and *stone* provide the reader with more information. Now we can make a stronger inference. It seems that her personality is cold, unfeeling, and as hard as stone.

Adjectives add more information in sentences. They help readers to better understand a writer's ideas. As a writer, you can use adjectives to help your readers better understand your ideas as well.

Review

Complete the sentence using different adjectives.

4.23) She was a(n) _____ flower in the summer heat.

4.24) He was a(n) _____ star, outshining all his peers.

4.25) The alarm clock is a(n) _____ commander, forcing me to wake up.

4.26) His song was a(n) _____ blanket of sounds making me feel warm inside.

Each sentence is a simile. Rewrite each sentence as a metaphor. Add in one adjective.

Example: Jeff ate like a wolf.
Jeff was a starving wolf.

4.27) The moon shined like a lantern in the sky.

_____

_____

4.28) Shannon sings like a nightingale.

_____

_____

4.29) The snow covered the ground like a blanket.

_____

_____

4.30) The baby's hair was as soft as silk.

_____

_____

4.31) He swam as fast and as gracefully as a dolphin.

_____

_____

 Teacher Check

30

5. LITERARY CONNECTIONS

MAKING LITERARY CONNECTIONS

Have you ever read a book and thought, "This sounds like something I have read in a book or seen on television"? That means that you were making comparisons. You made connections between the two books or the book and a television show. You noticed what was similar, and you probably also started to think about how the two were different. This is called contrasting. You recently read two books that seemed very different, but if you think about it, there are many similarities between them as well. In this Lesson, you will think about connections you can make between *In the Year of the Boar and Jackie Robinson* and *Dear Austin*.

First, you will answer a few questions about each story.

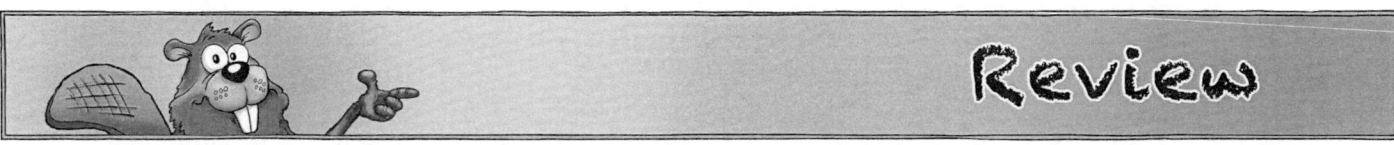

Copy and complete these sentences into your Reading Journal. Your answers will be based on your personal experience.

5.1)

> ### In the Year of the Boar and Jackie Robinson
> #### by Bette Bao Lord
>
> - I have read another book similar to this one. Yes or No?
> - This book is an example of _____ (genre).
> - The illustrations remind me of _____ (another book title or a place).
> - _____ took place in this same time or location (a historical event).

- Shirley reminds me of _____
_____ in another
book I read (character).
- The story's plot is similar to _____
_____ (book or
movie title).
- The lesson I learned in this book was
_____
(theme).
- This book is _____
(funny, sad, scary, intriguing, etc.).

5.2)

Dear Austin—Letters From the Underground Railroad
by Elvira Woodruff

- I have read another book similar to this one. Yes or No?
- This book is an example of _____
_____ (genre).
- The illustrations remind me of
_____ (another book
title or a place).
- _____ took place in this
same time or location (a historical event).
- Levi reminds me of _____
_____ in another
book I read (character).
- The story's plot is similar to _____
_____ (book or
movie title).
- The lesson I learned in this book was
_____
(theme).

● This book is _____
  (funny, sad, scary, intriguing, etc.).

Teacher Check

Connecting Your Ideas Between Texts

5.3) Complete the chart using what you learned from the two books you read. You do not need to complete the chart in complete sentences.

Books	What was the main character's main goals?	What was in the main character's way? How did the main character respond to this challenge?	What historical and/or significant events took place in the story?	What did you learn about the main characters? (character traits)	What are some important ideas presented in the book?
In the Year of the Boar and Jackie Robinson	a.	b.	c.	d.	e.
Dear Austin	f.	g.	h.	i.	j.

Both books: What is a message that both authors were trying to share with the reader?

m.

Teacher Check

COMPARE AND CONTRAST SHIRLEY AND LEVI.

Now, let's take a deeper look at one trait that Shirley and Levi share—their loyalty and friendships with their close friends. Levi's letters to his brother reveal his closeness to Jupiter. For example, although Jupiter does not talk, Levi can interpret his body language and gestures fluently. The boys show loyalty for one another through their actions. Levi decides to take a risky adventure with Jupiter to try to find Darcy in hostile and unfamiliar territory. They survive by trusting in one another as well as help from strangers.

Similarly, Shirley learns to develop her friendship with the most unlikely person—the tallest, strongest, and fastest girl in all of fifth grade, Mabel. Through their friendship, Shirley is accepted by the rest of her classmates. She also learns to play and love baseball. Through her love and knowledge of baseball, she learns the meaning of American spirit—that anyone can be anything if they believe. She also becomes friends with Emily Levy, a new girl. Shirley can empathize (understand what it feels like) with Emily as a new student. She welcomes Emily, and the two become fast friends. Through her friendships with both Emily and Mabel, Shirley learns about the true meaning of friendship—to sacrifice (give up something you love for someone else) selflessly.

5.4) Use the Venn diagram to show the similarities and differences between Shirley and Levi. The middle part of the Venn diagram should include information that both characters share (their similarities). List three characteristics each about Shirley and Levi, and then list three similarities they both share.

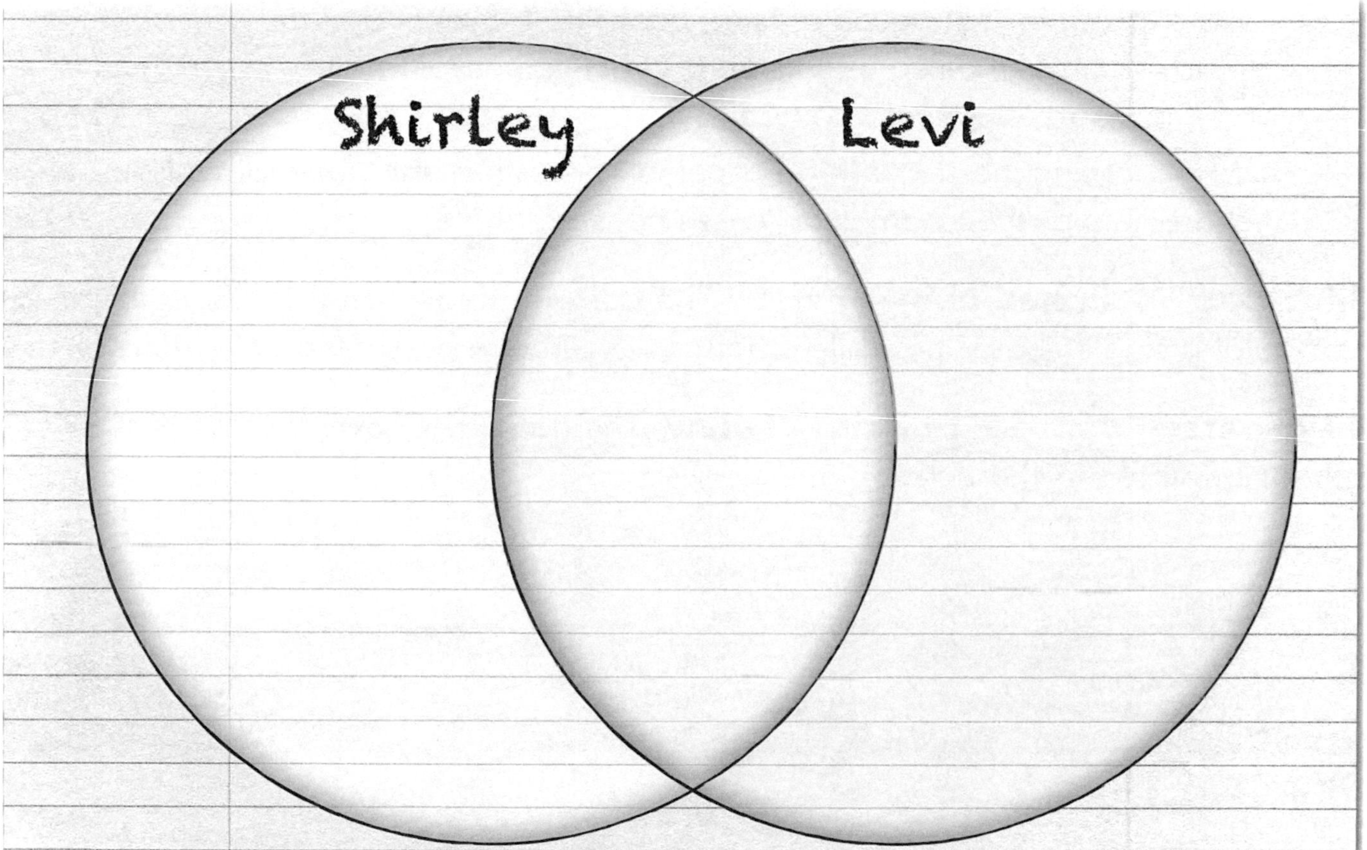

Shirley

Levi

NARRATOR'S POINT OF VIEW

In the beginning of this course, you were introduced to the narrator's point of view. To refresh your memory, let's do a quick review. Remember, the narrator or speaker is the one telling the story from a specific **point of view**. This point of view can be in first or third person.

First-person point of view: tells my story. The subject *I* or *we* is used.

> **Example**: ***I*** *went to school with my best friend.* ***We*** *always sit next to each other.*

Who is telling the story? In first-person narration, the narrator is *I* or *we*.

Third-person point of view: tells the story as someone who is outside of the story. The story is told as *he*, *she*, and *they*.

> **Example**: ***Nathan*** *loved playing basketball. Every day after school,* ***he*** *ran to the basketball court outside to practice basketball with his friends. When it got dark,* ***he*** *would go home.*

Who is telling the story? In third-person narration, the narrator calls the characters by their names and uses *he*, *she*, or *they*.

Third-person limited point of view: The narrator knows only the thoughts and feelings of a single character, while other characters are presented only externally.

Third-person omniscient point of view: The narrator knows the thoughts and feelings of all of the characters in the story.

Review

Choose the best answers.

5.5) _____ *In the Year of the Boar and Jackie Robinson* is written in ___ .
   A. first-person
   B. third-person limited
   C. third-person omniscient

5.6) _____ *Dear Austin—Letters From the Underground Railroad* is written in ___.
   A. first-person
   B. third-person limited
   C. third-person omniscient

5.7) _____ First-person narration uses the subjects ___.
   A. I
   B. we
   C. both A and B

5.8) _____ Third-person narration uses the subjects ___.
   A. he/she
   B. they
   C. both A and B

Check Correct Recheck

6. COMPARE AND CONTRAST ESSAY

Writing

COMPARE AND CONTRAST ESSAY

You have already learned about comparing and contrasting. You have compared and contrasted the two main characters of the books you read as well. Now, you should have enough information to write a five-paragraph compare and contrast essay. Today, you will begin writing an essay about the similarities and differences of Shirley and Levi. Use the chart and the Venn diagram you completed in Lesson 5 to help you. Your essay will include an introductory paragraph that states your main topic, three body paragraphs that support your main topic, and a conclusion paragraph.

Look at the hamburger model:

Hamburger Writing

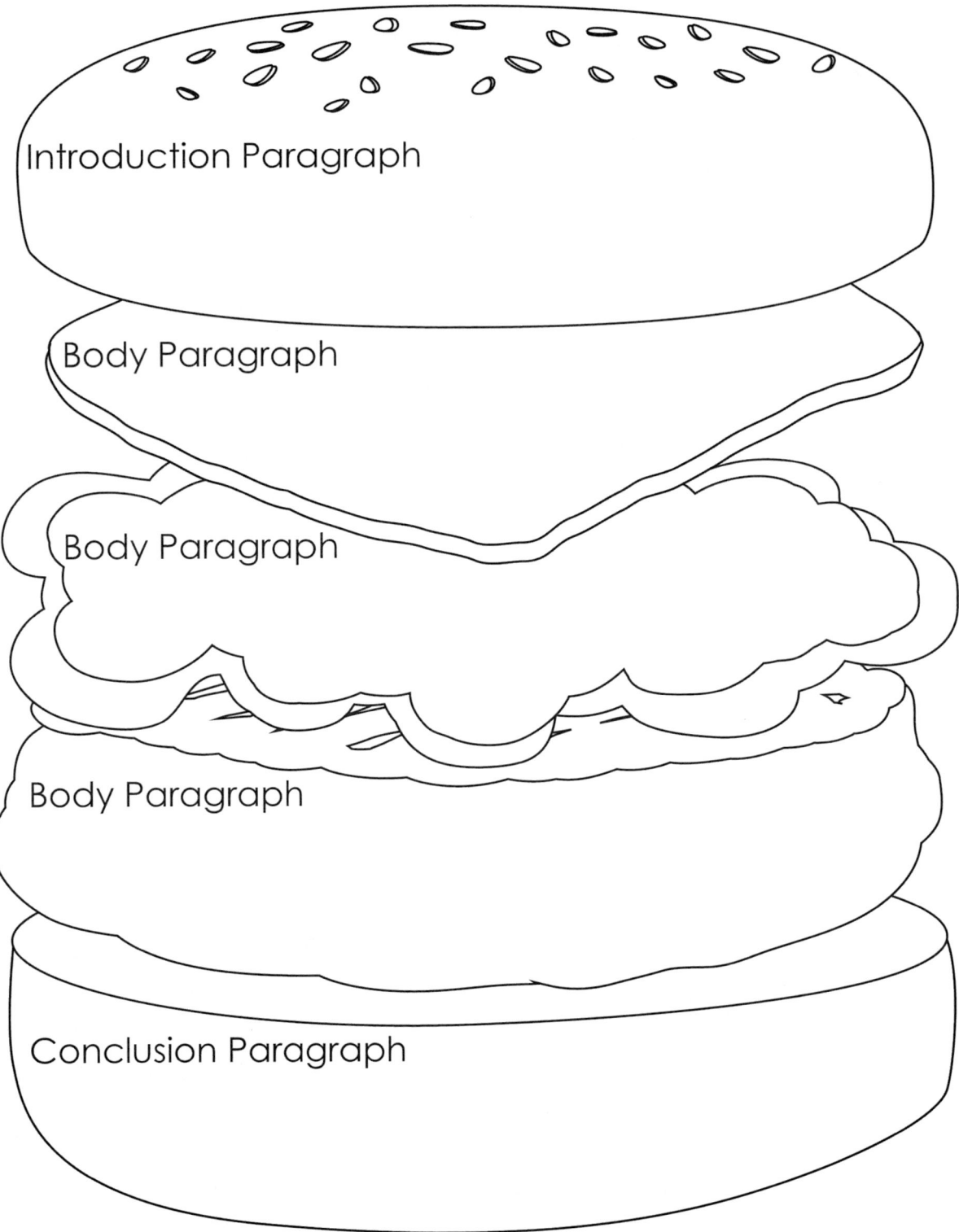

Introduction Paragraph

Body Paragraph

Body Paragraph

Body Paragraph

Conclusion Paragraph

The top bun is your introduction. Since you will be writing about the two main characters, Shirley and Levi, your topic sentence should be focused on them. Your introductory paragraph should include or do the following:

- a topic sentence that states the main idea of your essay

- a main idea supported by facts (from the books)

- a topic sentence that gives your own views (opinion) on the main idea

- have at least three sentences

Here are a couple of topic sentences you can use to help you get your essay started:

- *Although Shirley and Levi share many similarities, they are also very unique and different.*

- *Shirley and Levi are similar in many ways, but they are also very different.*

The cheese, lettuce, and patty represent the bodies of the essay. All of the three body paragraphs should have unity. This means each of the three paragraphs should all be related to the main idea stated in the topic sentence. Your body paragraphs should include the following:

☐ Each new paragraph should give some more information that helps support your topic sentence.

☐ Each new paragraph should have its own topic sentence.

☐ Try not to cram too much information into the body paragraphs. Do not include information that is unrelated to the topic sentence.

☐ Using transitional words or phrases will help the paragraphs flow from one to another.

- Compare transitional words: *similarly, like, as, also, likewise, just as, in the same way, in addition*

- Contrast transitional words: *however, on the other hand, but, in contrast, unlike, instead, on the contrary, in spite of, although*

*Use the Venn Diagram from Lesson 5 for information to include in your paragraphs.

To help you organize your essay, follow these suggested guidelines:

Body Paragraph 1 (the cheese):
- ☐ Write at least three sentences that are unique to Shirley.
- ☐ Use text evidence to support your topic sentence about Shirley.
- ☐ If using quotations, be sure to quote exactly as the text is written.

Body Paragraph 2 (the lettuce):
- ☐ Write at least three sentences that are unique to Levi.
- ☐ Use text evidence to support your topic sentence about Levi.
- ☐ If using quotations, be sure to quote exactly as the text is written.

Body Paragraph 3 (the patty):
- ☐ Write at least three sentences that show how Shirley and Levi are similar.
- ☐ Use text evidence to support your topic sentence about how they are similar.
- ☐ If using quotations, be sure to quote exactly as the text is written.

The bottom bun will make up the conclusion paragraph. This paragraph will sum up the essay. It should be interesting to the reader. Your conclusion should include or do the following:
- ☐ Restate or stress the main idea (from the introductory paragraph) in a different way.
- ☐ Mention the main point of each paragraph in an interesting or different way.
- ☐ Share with the reader something you learned, or state your opinion about the main topic.
- ☐ Do not add any new information to the conclusion paragraph.

Review

Now, take this time to compose your five-paragraph essay. Remember to visualize the writing of your essay as if constructing a hamburger. Here is some information to help guide you when writing your essay:

Focus

You must identify your topic in the introduction. Make sure your topic can be identified throughout your essay. (Remember, the purpose for your essay is to help your reader understand how Shirley and Levi are alike and different.)

Content

Your essay should demonstrate a clear understanding of both characters. You should be able to use text evidence to support your thoughts and opinions in your writing.

Organization

You should use transitional words to connect your sentences and paragraphs. Include a conclusion to sum up your essay.

Style/Voice

You should use precise and interesting word choices to share your ideas about the two characters.

Conventions

You should use a variety of sentences and vocabulary. Your essay should contain few, if any, errors. These errors should not interfere with the readers' understanding of your writing.

6.1) Write your compare and contrast essay.

_____

_____

_____

_____

_____

_____

_____

_____

_____

_____

_____

_____

_____

IT WAS A DARK AND STORMY NIGHT ...

QUIZ 2

(Each answer, 5 points)
Underline the words that best complete the similes.

2.01)   She limped like a(n) (**excited**, **bruised**) animal.

2.02)   Tony's voice boomed like a (**calm**, **noisy**) group of instruments.

2.03)   Shelly's smile filled the room like a (**bright**, **dull**) light.

2.04)   I felt rested because I slept like a (**grouchy**, **peaceful**) baby.

2.05)   Hummingbirds look like (**dazzling**, **boring**) jewels with bright colors.

Write T for True or F for False.

2.06)   _____ Third-person narration includes using the pronouns *I* and *we*.

2.07)   _____ First-person narration includes using the pronouns *I* and *we*.

Underline the forms of the words that best complete the sentences.

2.08)   How does lettuce (**differ**, **difference**) from spinach?

2.09)   We used information from our character trait diagrams to (**compare**, **comparison**) the two main characters.

2.010) The teacher said to include three (**similarity**, **similarities**) between lions and cheetahs in the paragraph.

2.011) I want to learn if this shampoo is (**similar**, **similarly**) to the one I use.

2.012) I noticed that my dog behaves (**difference**, **differently**) for me than she does for my sister.

Choose the correct spelling of each word.

2.013) _____   A. compairison
                B. comperison
                C. comparison

2.014) _____   A. different
                B. diffurent
                C. diferent

2.015) _____   A. differents
                B. diffurense
                C. difference

2.018) _____   A. difer
                B. differ
                C. diffur

2.016) _____   A. similerlie
                B. simlarley
                C. similarly

2.019) _____   A. compere
                B. compare
                C. compair

2.017) _____   A. similarity
                B. simlarity
                C. simlaritie

2.020) _____   A. differences
                B. diffurences
                C. diferences

Check ☐   Correct ☐   Recheck ☐

PICTURE THIS!

Wisdom is using truth to make daily choices. A wise person knows the truth and puts it into practice every day!

Imagine a jar full of marbles. Every time you make a good decision, it is like adding a marble to the jar. The more good decisions you make, the "wiser" you become. Each wrong or foolish decision is like taking a marble out, and slowly the jar becomes empty.

Every choice is important, including the friends you make, the books you read, the programs you watch, and how you spend your free time.

Apply good character to every decision!

Owl Mobile

Listen to my parents and teachers

Learn from correction

Choose my friends carefully

Remember that there are consequences to my actions

Ask, "What is the right thing to do?"

Supplies

- brown paper lunch sack
- brown, yellow, and blank paper
- red and black markers
- 5 feet of yarn
- scissors, glue, and clear tape
- pens or pencils

Instructions

Fill a brown paper sack with crumpled newspaper, and tape the sack closed. Cut wings and ears out of brown paper, then cut eyes and a mouth using yellow paper. Color the eyes with a black marker and color the mouth with a red marker. Tape the ears and wings to the sack, and glue the eyes and mouth in place.

Tape three, 1-foot lengths of yarn to the bottom of the sack. Write each "I Will" of wisdom on a small piece of blank paper, and tape the "I Wills" to the yarn. Tape another piece of yarn, about 2 feet long, to the top of the sack as a hanger.

SECTION THREE

OBJECTIVES

- Write detailed sentences.
- Understand how setting contributes to the plot of a story.
- Revise your compare and contrast essay.
- Edit your work and the work of others.
- Spell words that end with *–ure* correctly.
- Spell homophones correctly.
- Complete analogies using synonyms and antonyms.
- Publish your writing.

7. STRENGTHENING SENTENCES

STRENGTHENING YOUR SENTENCES USING DETAILS

When writing, you want to create strong, detailed sentences. You want to make sure to give the readers a lot of detail. Including many details helps to engage the reader, who will understand your ideas and connect with your writing. Here is a strategy to help you to write strong, detailed sentences.

Example 1: *My mom cooked my favorite meal.*

Add an adjective:

> *My **wonderful** mom cooked my favorite meal.*

Add an adverb:

> *My wonderful mom **happily** cooked my favorite meal.*

Add a prepositional phrase:

> *My wonderful mom happily cooked my favorite meal **for my birthday.***

Example 2: *The dog barked.*
    Add an adjective:
        *The **black and white** dog barked.*
    Add an adverb:
        *The black and white dog barked **viciously**.*
    Add one or more prepositional phrases:
        *The black and white dog barked viciously (**at me**) (**through the fence**).*

Review

Strengthen the sentences by following the instructions.

The boy sat.

7.1) Add one or more adjectives: _____

7.2) Add an adverb: _____

7.3) Add a prepositional phrase: _____

_____

The egg smelled.

7.4) Add one or more adjectives: _____

7.5) Add an adverb: _____

7.6) Add a prepositional phrase: _____

_____

The book fell.

7.7) Add one or more adjectives: _____

7.8) Add an adverb: _____

7.9) Add a prepositional phrase: _____

_____

My brother danced.

7.10) Add one or more adjectives: _____

7.11) Add an adverb: _____

7.12) Add a prepositional phrase: _____

_____

One of the vases broke.

7.13) Add one or more adjectives: _____

7.14) Add an adverb: _____

7.15) Add a prepositional phrase: _____

_____

Teacher Check ☐

HOW DOES THE SETTING HELP CONTRIBUTE TO THE PLOT?

The setting of a story is the time and place in which the story takes place. In most stories, setting is very important to the development of the plot. Setting can play a critical role in how the story progresses.

Without the setting, both of the stories you read, *In the Year of the Boar and Jackie Robinson* and *Dear Austin—Letters From the Underground Railroad*, could not have developed the way they did. Think about the way the setting affected the conflicts and the events in each book. Did the setting affect what the characters said? Did it affect the characters' actions?

The historical and cultural setting of a story means the time period in which the characters live. It also includes the customs, values, and beliefs of that time and place. Both of the stories you read were set in historically important times. In the book *In the Year of the Boar and Jackie Robinson*, the story went back and forth between the Chinese and American cultures. Shirley had to learn to strike a balance in her life. She had to live as an obedient Chinese daughter. At the same time, she had to understand how to live as an American student.

The story also occurred during an important time period in U.S. baseball history. Think about the real events that happened in 1947 that influenced the setting. The story could not have unfolded the way it did without some real events that happened. If the setting had been in a different U.S. city, the character of Shirley would not have known the significance of the Dodgers. Without the real-life person of Jackie Robinson, Shirley could not have made the connection of how he represented the American dream. Without the World Series happening, Mrs. Rappaport might not have told the students why baseball is "America's game."

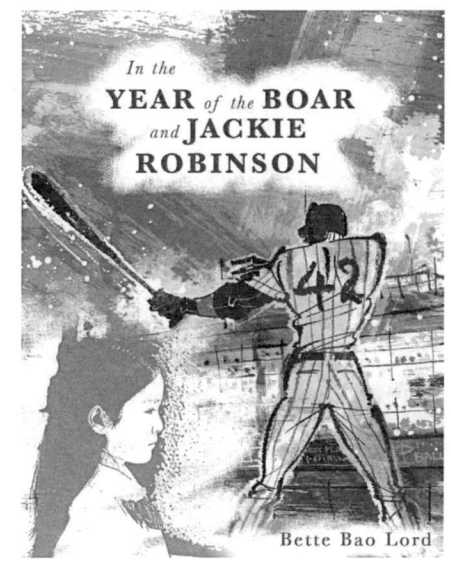

In *Dear Austin*, the historical and cultural setting also played a vital role in plot development. It is set in the year 1853. At the time, the people of the United States were fiercely divided about slavery. Because laws in the southern states still legalized slavery, Jupiter and Darcy were considered "property." Living as free citizens in Pennsylvania offered some protection for them, but events in the story created conflict for the characters. Without the story being set during this time period, the story would not have been able to develop the way it did. Levi would not have been able to know the significance of Harriet Tubman. The author may not have been able to introduce the importance of the Underground Railroad.

The Underground Railroad was a secret network of sympathetic whites and brave former slaves like Harriet Tubman who led groups of slaves to freedom. During this time period, it was culturally accepted by many whites to think that slaves were property instead of human beings. The character Levi learned that no matter what a person's skin color is, no one deserves to be considered a slave.

Can you see how real people and events of certain time periods may have influenced the settings of both stories? Can you see how the setting of both stories contributed to the plot development? How does the setting create conflict for Levi trying to save Darcy from the slave catchers? How does the setting create conflict for Shirley learning how to make friends and learning about baseball?

In your own words, answer the questions. Use text evidence from the books to support your answers.

7.16) How does the setting in *In the Year of the Boar and Jackie Robinson* affect the plot? Give at least two examples.

a. _____

_____

b. _____

_____

7.17) How does the setting in *Dear Austin—Letters From the Underground Railroad* affect the plot? Give at least two examples.

a. _____

_____

b. _____

_____

Teacher Check ☐

Writing

REVISE YOUR COMPARE AND CONTRAST ESSAY.

Today, you will revise your compare/contrast essay. Remember, during this part of the writing process, you do not need to worry about anything except the content of your writing. Focus on making your voice clear and easy to understand for your reader. Each of your paragraphs should support the main idea of your essay. Your sentences should be clear and concise (to the point). Your thoughts should be written in a logical order and flow seamlessly. Each paragraph should have a topic sentence and supporting sentences. The supporting sentences could be examples from the story, text evidence, facts, or your opinions about the book. Make sure you have included a variety of sentences. Some of your sentences should be short, and some should be longer. Did you use sensory words, adjectives, and figurative language? This is the time to strengthen and make your essay more interesting. You will edit and proof your essay in Lesson 8, so do not do that in today's Lesson.

Review

7.18) Revise your compare and contrast essay.

_____
_____
_____
_____
_____
_____
_____
_____
_____
_____
_____
_____
_____
_____
_____
_____
_____
_____

_____

_____

_____

_____

_____

_____

_____

_____

_____

_____

_____

_____

_____

_____

_____

_____

_____

_____

_____

_____

_____

_____

 Teacher Check ☐

8. EDITING EXERCISE

Writing

EDITING EXERCISE

This Lesson will give you some more practice with editing. You became familiar with the editing and proofing marks in Unit 3. A chart with those marks is included here.

Editing Symbols

Symbol	Meaning
⁋	Start a new paragraph.
sp. ⬭	Correct spelling.
∧	Insert a word, letter, or phrase.
⬭	Delete a letter, word, or group of words.
≡	Capitalize a letter.
/	Change to lower case.
∧	Insert punctuation.
⌄⌄ ⌄	Insert quotation marks or an apostrophe.
⊙	Insert end punctuation.
∫	Transpose (reverse) words or letters.
#	Insert a space.

54

Read the following paragraph. Watch for mistakes in capitalization, grammar, punctuation, and spelling.

(1) Lincoln and Charlie decided to play a game of Basketball during lunch. (2) Charlie asked Lincoln to get a ball from the gym. (3) Lincoln went to the gym but Coach Lambert was not there. (4) Lincoln knew where the basketballs were stored, but he didn't know if he should take one without permission. (5) What should he do. Coach Lambert might be angry if Lincoln took the ball without permission. (6) Time was passing. (7) Before long, it would be time to go back to class. (8) Lincoln guessed that Charlie and he just wouldn't be able to play basketball that day. (9) Just as Lincoln was about to leave the gym, coach Lambert appeared. (10) Lincoln asked may I use one of the basketballs during lunch. (11) Coach Lambert said, "Sure!" (12) The game was back on!

Choose the best answers based on the paragraph.

8.1) _____ What change, if any, should be made to sentence 1?
   A. Change *Lincoln* to *lincoln*.
   B. Change *Basketball* to *basketball*.
   C. Add a comma after *Basketball*.
   D. Make no changes.

8.2) _____ What change, if any, should be made to sentence 3?
   A. Add a comma after Lincoln.
   B. Add a comma after *gym*.
   C. Change *there* to *their*.
   D. Make no changes.

8.3) _____ What change, if any, should be made to sentence 5?
   A. Change the period to a question mark.
   B. Change *do* to *done*.
   C. Add a comma after *What*.
   D. Make no changes.

8.4) _____ What is the best way to rewrite sentences 6 and 7?
        A. *Time was passing, but before long it would be time to go back to class.*
        B. *Time was passing before long it would be time to go back to class.*
        C. *Time was passing, before long it would be time to go back to class.*
        D. Make no changes. The sentences are correct.

8.5) _____ Which of the following is the best way to correct sentence 10?
        A. *Lincoln asked, "May I use one of the basketballs during lunch"?*
        B. *Lincoln asked, "May I use one of the basketballs during lunch?"*
        C. *Lincoln asked, "may I use one of the basketballs during lunch?"*
        D. Make no changes. The sentence is correct.

EDITING YOUR OWN ESSAY

In today's Lesson, you will edit your compare and contrast essay. Remember, just like in the exercise that you just completed, you will take the time to find all your grammatical and spelling errors. This is the time to polish and clean up your paragraphs.

8.6) Use the Editing Symbols chart to edit and proof your own essay.

Read each spelling word out loud.

8.7) Write the spelling words five times each on separate paper.

creature	**departure**
furniture	**fracture**
structure	**culture**
pressure	**signature**
treasure	**fixture**

Note: You will be tested on all of the spelling words during the Unit Test.

Teacher Check

Unscramble the spelling words.

8.8) t u t s u r e r c   _____

8.9) s p r e r s u e   _____

8.10) r a s t u e r e   _____

8.11) t s i u n a r e g   _____

8.12) r t u r n i u e f   _____

8.13) r e r p a t u e d   _____

8.14) r e l c u t u   _____

8.15) u a c e t r e r   _____

8.16) i u t x r e f   _____

8.17) r c a f e r u t   _____

Write the spelling words in alphabetical order.

departure	creature	furniture	treasure	fracture
structure	pressure	signature	fixture	culture

8.18) _____

8.19) _____

8.20) _____

8.21) _____

8.22) _____

8.23) _____

8.24) _____

8.25) _____

8.26) _____

8.27) _____

Check   Correct   Recheck

9. HOMOPHONES, SYNONYMS, AND ANTONYMS

Language

MORE HOMOPHONES

Homophones are words that sound the same but are spelled differently and have different meanings. Knowing homophones helps you to better understand what you read. Using homophones correctly will improve your writing as well. Here are a few more examples of homophones. If you do not know the meaning of a word, look it up in the dictionary.

chews	choose
steal	steel
your	you're
cymbal	symbol
brake	break

58

Match the pictures with the homophones.

9.1) _____

9.2) _____ It's ___ birthday!

A. chews

B. choose

C. steal

D. steel

E. cymbal

F. symbol

G. brake

H. break

I. your

J. you're

9.3) _____

9.4) _____

9.5) _____

9.6) _____

9.7) _____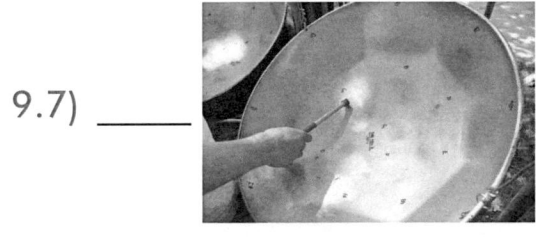

9.8) _____

9.9) _____

9.10) _____

Check   Correct   Recheck

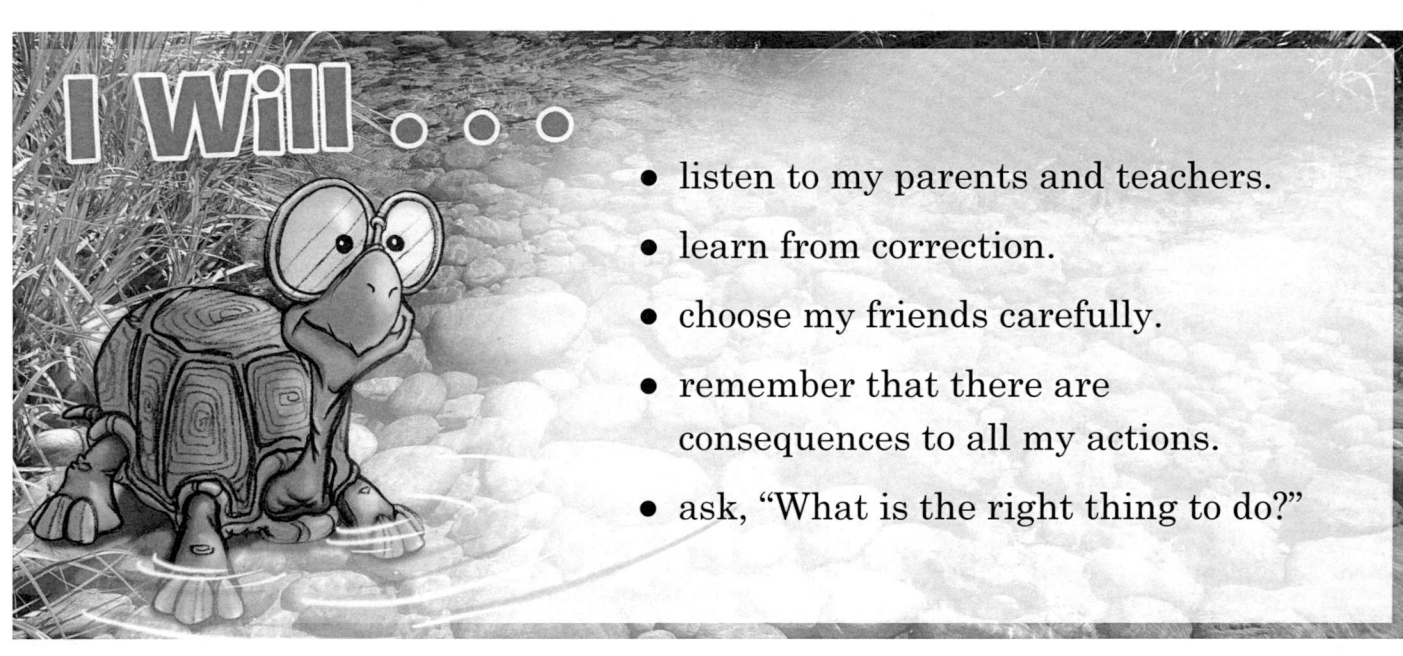

I Will...

- listen to my parents and teachers.
- learn from correction.
- choose my friends carefully.
- remember that there are consequences to all my actions.
- ask, "What is the right thing to do?"

60

MORE SYNONYMS AND ANTONYMS

Understanding the meanings of prefixes and suffixes can help you identify and create antonyms. Remember that antonyms are words that have opposite or different meanings from each other.

Language

The suffixes *-ful* and *-less* are opposites of each other. You can add these suffixes to words to create antonyms.

The suffix *-ful* means full of, characterized by, or able to.

thought	+	*ful*	= thoughtful (characterized by thoughts)
care	+	*ful*	= careful (full of care)
shame	+	*ful*	= shameful (characterized by or full of shame)
harm	+	*ful*	= harmful (able to harm)

The suffix *-less* means without or failure or inability to perform or be performed.

thought	+	*less*	= thoughtless (without thought)
care	+	*less*	= careless (without care)
shame	+	*less*	= shameless (without shame)
harm	+	*less*	= harmless (inability to harm)

The prefixes *un-* and *im-* mean *not*. You can add them to words and make antonyms.

un	+	clean	= unclean (not clean)
un	+	fair	= unfair (not fair)
un	+	told	= untold (not told)
im	+	possible	= impossible (not possible)
im	+	mature	= immature (not mature)
im	+	patient	= impatient (not patient)

Apply what you've learned to help you complete the following antonym analogies.

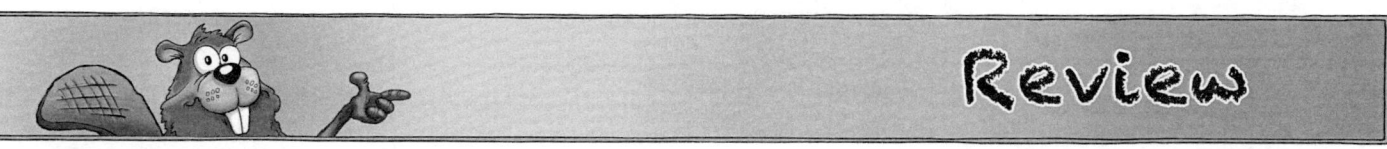

Review

Complete each analogy using the prefixes *im-* and *un-* or the suffixes *-ful* and *-less*.

9.11) joyful : joyless   :: patient : _____

9.12) fair : unfair   :: comfortable : _____

9.13) kind : unkind   :: colorful : _____

9.14) blameful : blameless :: proper : _____

9.15) pure : impure   :: cheer : _____

SUBMIT YOUR ESSAY

Congratulations! You have prepared, written, revised, and edited your compare and contrast essay. You are now ready to publish your written work. Make sure you create a title that shows the message of your essay as well. Include your name and date.

NOTE: The compare and contrast essay counts as 40% of the Quiz 3 grade.

9.16) Submit a clean copy of your essay to your teacher.

COMPARE AND CONTRAST ESSAY RUBRIC

	Exemplary 4 Points	Accomplished 3 Points	Developing 2 Points	Beginning 1 Point	Point Tally
Focus	The topic is clearly identified throughout the writing, including the introductory section.	The topic is moderately identified throughout the writing, including the introductory section.	There is some evidence of a topic throughout, and/or there is no introduction.	The topic is weak, and there is no introduction.	_____

Content	The topic is well-developed through relevant facts and details about the characters.	The topic is moderately developed through relevant facts and details about the characters.	There is some evidence of relevant facts and details about the characters.	There are little or no relevant facts and details about the characters.	_____
Organization	Information clearly connects through transitional words and phrases with a concluding section.	Information moderately connects through transitional words and phrases with a concluding section.	Some information connects through grouping and/ or is missing a concluding section.	Little or no information connects logically or through grouping, and there is no concluding section.	_____
Style/Voice	The topic is clearly explained through precise word choice.	The topic is moderately explained through precise word choice.	Some of the topic is explained through precise word choice.	There is minimal use of precise word choice.	_____
Conventions	The essay has grade-level appropriate spelling, grammar, and punctuation; it contains few or no errors that interfere with the reader's understanding.	The essay has mainly grade-level appropriate spelling, grammar, and punctuation; it contains 1–2 errors that do not interfere with the reader's understanding.	The essay may contain 3–4 errors in spelling, grammar, and/ or punctuation that may interfere with the reader's understanding.	The essay may contain frequent and numerous errors (5+) in spelling, grammar, and punctuation that interfere with the reader's understanding.	_____
				Total Points =	_____
Grade (The compare and contrast essay counts as 40% of the Quiz 3 grade.)				**Total Points (_____) × 2 =**	_____/40

I will listen to my parents,
And I'll hear my teachers, too.
I'll remember there's a consequence
To everything I do.

I will learn from their correction,
And I'll choose my friends with care.
I will stay away from foolishness
That only brings a snare.

STORY CLIMAX

QUIZ 3

NOTE: The compare and contrast essay counts as 40% of the Quiz 3 grade.

(Each answer, 5 points)
Choose the best answers.

3.01) _____ *The red and black snake curled calmly <u>around the tree branch</u>.*
Identify the underlined phrase used to make this sentence more descriptive.
A. adjective
B. adverb
C. prepositional phrase
D. none of these

3.02) _____ *My sweet baby sister laughed <u>gleefully</u> at me!*
Identify the underlined word used to make this sentence more descriptive.
A. adjective
B. adverb
C. prepositional phrase
D. none of these

Write T for True or F for False.

3.03) _____ The setting of a story can play an important role in the development of a story's plot.

Choose the best answers.

3.04) _____ The opposite of the suffix *–less* is ___.
A. *–more*
B. *–er*
C. *–est*
D. *–ful*

3.05) _____ unfair : fair :: ___ : patient
A. unpatient
B. impatient
C. inpatient
D. patientless

66

Write a homophone for each of the bolded words.

3.06) *He takes a risk to **steal** third base.*

_____

3.07) *Doris did not mean to **break** the delicate necklace chain.*

_____

Read the paragraph. Choose the best answers based on the paragraph.

(1) Micah rode his bike furiously up the hill He reached the top and stopped to catch his breath. (2) That was the fastest he had ever gone up that dreaded hill. (3) He made it? (4) He pumped his fist in the air in triumph.

3.08) _____ Which of the following is the best way to correct sentence 1?
  A. Micah rode his bike furiously up the hill and he reached the top and stopped to catch his breath.
  B. Micah rode his bike. Furiously up the hill and he reached the top. He stopped to catch his breath.
  C. Micah rode his bike furiously up the hill. He reached the top and stopped to catch his breath.
  D. Make no changes. The sentence is correct.

3.09) _____ Which of the following is the best way to correct sentence 3?
  A. He made it.
  B. He made it!
  C. He made it and he pumped his fist in the air in triumph.
  D. Make no changes. The sentence is correct.

Choose the correct spelling of each word.

3.010) _____ A. frakture   B. fracture   C. frackshure

3.011) _____ A. signachure   B. singature   C. signature

3.012) _____ A. fruniture   B. furniture   C. furnichure

Check ☐   Correct ☐   Recheck ☐

STOP and prepare for the Unit Practice Test.
- Review the Objectives and the Vocabulary.
- Reread the questions from each Lesson.
- Review the Quizzes.

PRACTICE TEST

(Each question, 4 points)
Choose the vocabulary words that best complete the sentences.

1) _____ My grandfather is amazed at the advancement in ___ when it comes to televisions.
   A. monologue
   B. prescription
   C. dialogue
   D. transcribe
   E. technology

2) _____ The boy stood with his ear to the door trying to listen to the ___ between his mom and grandma about Christmas presents.
   A. monologue
   B. prescription
   C. dialogue
   D. transcribe
   E. technology

3) _____ My doctor gave me a ___ for medicine to help me get over the flu.
   A. monologue
   B. prescription
   C. dialogue
   D. transcribe
   E. technology

4) _____ The court reporter's job is to ___ what is said during the trial.
   A. monologue
   B. prescription
   C. dialogue
   D. transcribe
   E. technology

Choose the forms of the words that best complete the sentences.

5) _____ The boys were arguing over who was the ___ in the class.
   A. taller
   B. tallest

6) _____ My wife has ___ handwriting than I do.
   A. prettier
   B. prettiest

7) _____ Michael Jordan is known as the ___ basketball player ever.
       A. greater
       B. greatest

8) _____ Jenny's hot sauce is ___ than Courtney's hot sauce.
       A. milder
       B. mildest

Match the idioms with the descriptions.

9) _____ beat around the bush

10) _____ through thick and thin

11) _____ Two wrongs don't make a right.

12) _____ When it rains, it pours.

A. to go through good times and bad times

B. Something that starts out as a little bit of trouble turns into a disaster.

C. when someone is avoiding the main point in a conversation

D. You cannot correct one wrong thing by doing something else that is wrong.

Choose the words that best complete the similes.

13) _____ His calf muscle tensed up until it was as hard as a ___.
       A. pillow
       B. rock

14) _____ The stars were sparkling like ___ last night.
       A. coal
       B. diamonds

15) _____ My friend, Jason, can run as fast as a ___.
       A. deer
       B. turtle

Write P if the underlined word is a Preposition, ADV for ADVerb, or ADJ for ADJective.

16) _____ The dog chased the cat <u>around</u> the yard all day.

17) _____ My brother and I crept <u>secretly</u> down the stairs.

Choose the best answers based on the paragraph.

(1) Curtis and Chad inched toward the starting point in the race. (2) Both were experienced runners. Especially at long distances. (3) The only question. Was which one would win the race this time. (4) As they raced to the finish line, giving it every bit of energy they had. The crowd hushed with silence. (5) It was a photo finish.

18) _____ Which of the following is the best way to correct sentence 2?
    A. Both were experienced runners especially. At long distances.
    B. Both were. Experienced runners especially at long distances.
    C. Both were experienced runners, especially at long distances.

19) _____ Which of the following is the best way to correct sentence 3?
    A. The only question was which one would win the race this time.
    B. The only question was. Which one would win the race this time.
    C. The only question was which one would. Win the race this time.

20) _____ Which of the following is the best way to correct sentence 4?
    A. As they raced. To the finish line, giving it every bit of energy they had.
    B. As they raced to the finish line, giving it every bit of energy they had, the crowd hushed with silence.
    C. As they raced to the finish line giving it every bit of energy. They had the crowd hushed with silence.

21) _____ Which of the following is the best way to correct sentence 5?
    A. It was a photo finish!
    B. It was. A photo finish.
    C. It was a photo finish?

Choose the correct spelling of each word.

22) _____
   A. similerlie
   B. simlarley
   C. similarly

23) _____
   A. compere
   B. compare
   C. compair

24) _____
   A. differents
   B. diffurense
   C. difference

25) _____
   A. signature
   B. signatore
   C. signitour

Check ☐   Correct ☐   Recheck ☐

You must now prepare for the Unit Test.
- Review the Objectives and the Vocabulary.
- Reread the questions from each Lesson.
- Review and study the Quizzes and Unit Practice Test.

When you are ready, turn in your Unit and request your Unit Test.